Mr Fudge

The Naughtiest Dog Ever

Sarah Reynold

Copyright © 2021 by Sarah Reynold
All rights reserved. No part of this publication may be reproduced, stored in any form of retrieval system or transmitted in any form or by any means without prior permission in writing from the publishers except for the use of brief quotations in a book review.

Dedication

This book is dedicated to George Skinner and his team at Edgemoor Veterinary Practice.

George is the best veterinarian I've ever known. His dedication came across with the work he did with small animals; he took the time to listen and explain the things I did not understand. George always showed kindness and empathy, including with the little things he did, which put me at ease when my animals were unwell. I would class him as a good friend.

George Skinner

Also, I dedicate this book to the man I love so much and am honoured to call my husband. Eddie has stood by my side throughout my heartbreak and supported me during one of the hardest times of my life.

Contents

Chapter 1. Puppy Home 10

Chapter 2. The Introduction of George 17

Chapter 3. Behind Enemy Lines 20

Chapter 4. Digging in the Garden 23

Chapter 5. Puppy Training 25

Chapter 6. Muzzle Training 28

Chapter 7. The Time He Lost His Manhood 29

Chapter 8. Eddie's Lack of Training 32

Chapter 9. Mr Fudge's boyfriend 34

Chapter 10. Travelling in the Car with the Crate 36

Chapter 11. The Friendship Between Mr Fudge and Auntie Fo 38

Chapter 12. Mr Fudge's First Christmas 40

Chapter 13. Discovery of Kong Toys for Dogs 44

Chapter 14. Mr Fudge, the Andrex Dog 45

Chapter 15. Mr Fudge and His Freckles 46

Chapter 16. Mr Fudge Turns One Year Old 47

Chapter 17. Family Visit 48

Chapter 18. Wedding Plans 49

Chapter 19. Mr Fudge Chewing Through His Harness 54

Chapter 20. My Hairdresser 55

Chapter 21. Mr Fudge's First Holiday and Our Honeymoon 56

Chapter 22. The Isle of Mull 61

Chapter 23. Learning How to Knit 66

Chapter 24. Mr Fudge Comfort Suckling 68

Chapter 25. No More Cushions 70

Chapter 26. Charlotte the Vet 71

Chapter 27. Bugs in His Lugs 72

Chapter 28. Mr Fudge Becomes Unwell 74

Chapter 29. Trying to Clean the House 76

Chapter 30. I Can't Believe It – He's Four Years Old! 77

Chapter 31. Mr Fudge's Trying to Hump My Arm 78

Chapter 32. Deciding on the New Shed 80

Chapter 33. Holiday to Dover and Mr Fudge's Most Stressful Time 83

Chapter 34. Keeping Mr Fudge Well and George's Retirement 91

Chapter 35. George's Retirement Day 93

Chapter 36. Finding a New Vets 95

Epilogue. Where We Are Now: Mr Fudge Is Nine Years Old 98

About the Author 104

Prologue

The year 2011.

At this time in my life, it was very stressful, and I had a lot of issues going on with my daughters. One of them was pregnant, and the other had flown the nest and was getting involved with the wrong kind of people. Emily, the eldest, ended up in prison, and Kate had tried her hardest to get pregnant since she was 16 years old.

Kate gave birth to twin boys, but they ended up in foster care and were then put up for adoption, as she had too many problems and issues to be able to look after them herself. Kate would have caused too much interference and disruption, so to give the boys a chance of a good life, I had to let them go for adoption rather than taking them on myself.

I also lost my two beautiful little Yorkshire Terriers, One had gone blind and given up at the age of 15, and the other was 16 and had cancer. They both got put to sleep in January of this year; it was a very hard year for me.

At this time, I was 42, and my partner Edward, Eddie for short, was 45.

Eddie was quite shy and quiet, but he was coming out of his shell slowly living with me. He said he wanted to wait at least six months before we got another dog. All he heard

Prologue

from me was "I need a dog," which went on for five and a half months. I felt there was something missing from our home, and he finally gave in, so I started the search for a new dog.

I knew someone who had a Jack Russell called Cherry. She was an old dog, but I fell in love with her, and then I knew what breed I wanted. A friend of mine, Anna, give me the names of some websites to start looking for a puppy. I found a breeder not far from where we lived and rang to see if they had any puppies. The man said he had just sold the last one but thought his other bitch had just been caught, so if I could ring back in about five weeks' time, he would know what was happening. I put his number in my phone under the name, "Jack Russell man."

Five weeks had passed, and I rang to see what was happening. He said that she was pregnant and they would be due in around 3 to 4 weeks. He would give me a ring and let me know when they had been born.

Jack Russell man rang to say the pups were here; there were three boys and one girl. I said I would be round as soon as I could, and it was four days later when I went to see them. I said I wanted a dog, not a bitch, as my previous bitch had been my baby girl, and I did not want to try and replace her.

Jack Russell man brought me the three dog pups to look

at and choose from. The one I chose was all white except for his tan markings, which were a big round spot around his tail, one on each side, and a v marking on his head and ears and down the right side of his face. Jack Russell man said, what happens if I change my mind?

Eddie replied, "she won't."

We left the house and talked of names. I said to Eddie that he looked like "Beethoven," the St. Bernard from the films.

Eddie said, "I'm not calling the dog Beethoven."

So I said, "Fine, you choose his name then", and Eddie came up with the name "Fudge", which I liked.

I went to work the next day and said, "I've chosen the puppy and his name is Fudge", showing them a photo of him on my phone.

A few weeks passed, and I rang the Jack Russell man to see if we could come and visit so Fudge would have an idea of who we are and learn to recognise our scent; we took him a blue puppy collar to wear.

Jack Russell man brought out all four puppies, and the little girl just cuddled into me.

I know they say that the puppy chooses you, but I think I picked the naughtiest one ever. All he did was attack Eddie's shoes and my fingers. He didn't want to be on my knee for cuddles; he just wanted to attack Eddie's shoes and laces and my trainers. He even got his brothers involved

Prologue

doing the same thing - attacking our shoes.

When I saw Fudge, he looked so fat, like an old banker from films, so his name became "Mr Fudge."

I went to my vets to inform them of the new puppy, get him registered and explained that we would be picking him up in around two weeks.

I then heard from social services that a couple had agreed to adopt my twin grandsons, and we arranged a visit to see the boys for the last time.

I used to ring their foster carer on a Sunday to see how the boys were getting on, as they had been born prematurely. I saw the boys for around a week on each visit, as they were a couple of hours away from where we were living, so we organised time off work and booked into a B&B nearby.

During the year, we had many conversations with social services about my grandchildren and what would be best for the boys. We went to see them in July, which would be the last time we would get to see and spend time with them. It was the saddest time in my life, but I knew this was the only way I could give them a settled life. Even though it was July, we asked the foster carer if we could have their first proper and our last Christmas with them this week. The foster carer said, of course, they are your grandchildren, and it would be lovely for the boys.

Chapter 1.
Puppy Home

At the end of the week that we had arranged we would pick up Mr Fudge, we had everything that we needed for him ready. He was so perfect and loved running all around the house and garden. But my God, we definitely knew we had him home; he was into everything! We had got him all kinds of puppy toys, but his favourites were a blue material duck, and a squeaky doughnut, both of which were filled with stuffing.

In our house, we had a corner suite that Mr Fudge used to run round in circles, even going behind it along the side of the wall. Within an hour, we heard clunk, clunk, clunk, coming from behind the settee. I looked over it to see what Mr Fudge was doing; he was only chewing on the electric cables for the lamp we had behind the corner suite! We quickly pulled out the settee and got Mr Fudge out, then blocked off each end of the corner suite with whatever we could find to stop him from getting behind.

Mr Fudge then decided he would go behind the TV stand and attack the wires and cables with his little sharp

Chapter 1. Puppy Home

puppy teeth. Not wanting him to hurt himself or cause any damage, I picked the cables up, and he bit my tit, causing me to yelp with pain. Little git! Mr Fudge had left little puncture marks underneath my tit, Eddie cleaned it up, and it was okay after that; not too painful.

I took the first week that we had him off work to help him settle in. Eddie and I tried to set some ground rules, e.g. Eddie didn't want the dog in the bed, so we agreed Mr Fudge would sleep downstairs in our kitchen/dining room. That was fine at first - until he started to cry at around 2 o'clock in the morning. Then Eddie or I would bring him and his puppy bed upstairs to our room, and he would sleep in that, at the side of our bed, until Eddie got up to get ready to go to work at around 6 o'clock. He would feed Mr Fudge his breakfast and let him in the garden to get clean, which is the command we taught him for relieving himself.

Before leaving for work, Eddie would put Mr Fudge on the bed and kiss me goodbye. I would fall back asleep and wake up a couple of hours later to find Mr Fudge's tail poking out of the quilt while the rest of him was underneath.

The second week, I was back at work, so Eddie took the week off work. The same thing happened, with Mr Fudge ending up sleeping in the bedroom, with his bed on the floor beside us. Normally when we went to bed, he would have a daft 5 minutes, running round and round and under the bed before settling down.

One day while we were watching TV in bed, we heard a rustling noise under the bed. Looking down, Eddie couldn't see Mr Fudge, so he got out of bed and looked underneath it. He discovered Mr Fudge happily chewing away at some cardboard storage boxes under the bed, which he had chewed large holes in, so everything stored underneath had to be moved to a new, safe location.

Mr Fudge when he was six weeks old.

Chapter 1. Puppy Home

Mr Fudge having a nap surrounded by various toys.

Mr Fudge loved chewing old trainers.

Laid at our back door with his rope bone.

Enjoying playing with his squeaky doughnut.

Chapter 1. Puppy Home

As a puppy, he seemed to enjoy sleeping in the most unusual positions.

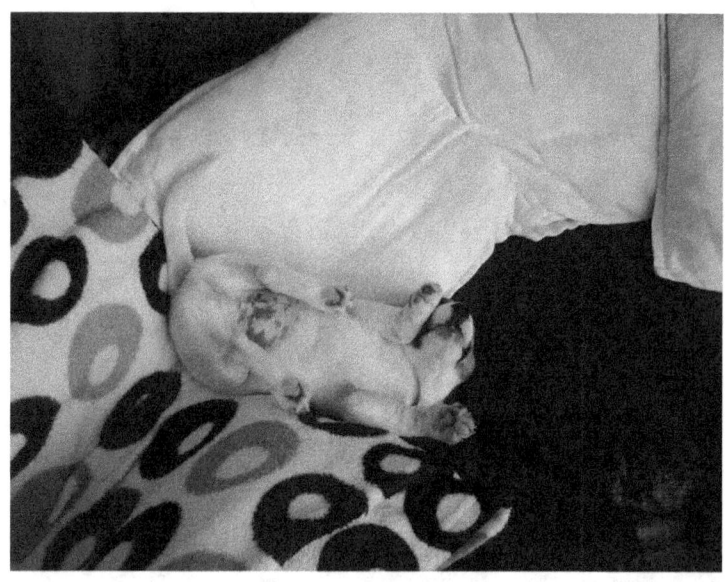

Having a nap in his usual position - on his back with his legs in the air.

Chapter 2.
The Introduction of George

When Mr Fudge was due to have his second vaccination a couple of weeks later, I took him to meet George, the best vet that I've ever known. I carried Mr Fudge in my arms into the vets as I did not drive at this time, and they had a surgery about a 15-minute walk from where we live. Mr Fudge saw a couple over my shoulder, and he was trying his hardest to escape my arms to go and see this couple. My arms were all over the place, trying to hold him with him wriggling and squirming everywhere. The couple were laughing so much that when they caught us up, they stopped to say hello, which pleased Mr Fudge.

As I've mentioned before, I previously had two little Yorkshire terriers. The girl had skin cancer and a lot of other issues going on with her, and the boy, who we nicknamed "little legs" as he was tiny, had gone blind a couple of years earlier and was starting to give up; he didn't have much quality of life.

This was when I discovered George the vet. We went to him for a second opinion on my baby girl; sometimes in life, people and a dog are just meant to be together. That's the way it was for me and my baby girl; little legs was just happy to be on anybody's knee to be cuddled and made a fuss of. George said we would know when the time was right to think about putting them to sleep, but at first, his opinion was it was too soon, and with his help, we shared another couple of years with them.

Eventually, I could tell that my baby girl was ready to go, and knew that little legs wouldn't cope alone without her. I made the decision the time was right to put them both to sleep. I was devastated, and the other things going on in my life didn't help. I rang George and said,

"I think it's time for them to go",

as my baby girl had curled up into a ball and was just telling us the time had come to let them go.

We had an appointment to see George, and I said I couldn't be in the room when he put them to sleep. George said he would just knock them out first while I was out of the room, then he would call us back in, and they would go to sleep in our arms for us to say our goodbyes. George injected both of them in the neck. I held my baby girl, and Eddie held little legs as they drifted off to sleep; we were both very upset. George had another appointment, but he saw them in the waiting room as we said our final goodbyes. We arranged for them to be cremated, and we

Chapter 2. The Introduction of George

still have their ashes at home.

George gave Mr Fudge his injection and said he was in good health and that he was so cute. He then said to Mr Fudge;

"you are one of the luckiest puppies to have such a really good home".

I walked away from the vets thinking what a nice thing for him to say.

Chapter 3.
Behind Enemy Lines

As Mr Fudge would not give up trying to chew on the wires behind the TV, we had to find a way to try and stop him. We have a square bay window, so Eddie thought to try and put up some green plastic garden fencing, which covered the space and would stop him from getting behind. It took up a bit of room, but would hopefully solve the problem. It became known as "behind enemy lines."

I don't know how Mr Fudge learned his name because he was called every name under the sun: "fucking little bastard," "fucking little twat," "little bastard," "little cunt," "little fucker."

Mr Fudge went to see George the vet for a check-up.

I said, "This dog is not normal; he's possessed!"

George just laughed and said it was typical of the breed. I said no, I've had many dogs in my lifetime but not one like Mr Fudge. He was around 12 weeks old at this point, though he was going for walks, and he always loved to walk with me. However, when I was not there, and Eddie tried to walk him, he never got any further than the end of our

Chapter 3. Behind Enemy Lines

path without picking him up. I mentioned this to George, just on the off-chance, and he said he was my dog, but I should take him for a little walk and let Eddie take him on big, longer walks.

Mr Fudge was so naughty in the things that he did; every day was something different. I was on a day off when he was playing in the dining room. He came to the door, and I saw he had some black mesh in his mouth, which he was chewing and chomping on. I jumped on him, but he had swallowed it before I could grab it; I didn't have a clue what it was.

I rang the vet straight away, and we were lucky to get an appointment with George. I explained what I had seen and said I had no idea of what it was; he said to keep an eye on him to make sure he was okay.

The next day, when Eddie was off work, and Mr Fudge was under the dining room table, he heard, click, click, click. Eddie went to see what was making the strange noise; it was only Mr Fudge attacking the webbing underneath the dining room chairs. When Eddie showed me, I knew this is what he had been chewing the day before, so Eddie had to remove all the webbing from the dining room chairs.

About three weeks later, I came in from work after doing an early shift. I finished around 2:30 in the afternoon and got home around 3 o'clock to find Mr Fudge had eaten all the stuffing out of his puppy bed. There was no stuffing left; he had eaten the lot.

On days we were both out at work, Eddie's dad would pop round during the day to see Mr Fudge, let him out in the garden to get clean and have a bit of play with him. He had even been around to check on him around 11 o'clock that day. I couldn't believe it!

I rang the vets to say what he'd done and again got an appointment to see them. This time, he saw a vet called Charlotte; she checked him over and said to keep an eye on him as he seems okay. Mr Fudge took an instant liking to Charlotte.

We give Mr Fudge old blankets for his bed now rather than buying a new one with stuffing for him to destroy and eat.

A few weeks later I again came home from work to discover he had eaten half of a red and black striped blanket; I couldn't believe it! I was again on the phone ringing the vets. The same thing was said; keep an eye on him as he seems to be fine.

Chapter 4.
Digging in the Garden

Eddie's dad used to come round and cut the grass for us in the summer. One day he'd cut the grass and was doing a little planting in some pots, whilst behind him, Mr Fudge decided to dig a huge hole. All the while, Eddie's dad didn't notice. I was working a 14-hour shift then sleeping in at work, followed by another 14-hour shift the next day, Eddie got home from work about 5 pm; he couldn't believe it, the size of this hole in the lawn.

The next day Eddie's dad, who, by the way, is named Brian, came round to see to Mr Fudge, and he saw the huge hole that Mr Fudge had dug the day before. When Eddie got in later that day from work, his dad rang him and said about the hole. Eddie laughed and said that

"Mr Fudge did that yesterday while you were looking after him".

Brian just laughed out loud and said

"I didn't notice a thing."

When I got in from work at 9:30 pm, Eddie told me about the hole and what Brian had said. We had a chat, and

I came up with the suggestion that we would get Mr Fudge a sandpit so he could have somewhere to dig without destroying the lawn. We found one in a shop, built it and put sand in it, but Mr Fudge would not even go in it. So I came up with another idea to try hiding biscuits in the sand.

If you think of a dog digging, you imagine he would use his paws very gently to uncover the biscuit then eat it. That is all Mr Fudge ever did in his sandbox. We tried so hard to get him to dig in it, but he was so cunning that he just got the biscuits out then waited for more.

Enjoying the summer sunshine in our back garden.

Chapter 5.
Puppy Training

In the 12 weeks that we had had Mr Fudge, he was trained to go in the garden and was a very clean dog. He used to come and sit and lift up one of his paws all on his own, so I just put the words in sit and paw. Doing this, he soon picked up the command of sit and paw, and I also taught him the commands stay and wait.

Mr Fudge would nip at my sleeves or my arms; I did not have a top that didn't have holes in it and had bruises all over my arms when he couldn't get his own way.

Talking to George the vet, he would just laugh and say yet again it was the breed. I would disagree and say yet again this dog is possessed; it's not right. George suggested that we should try a dog psychologist and suggested one he knew. Her name was Moira, so we organised for her to visit us.

When she first came through the door, Mr Fudge weed on the wood flooring right in front of her. Moira said that's because he was excited she was here; Eddie and I just looked at each other thinking, yeah, whatever. She handed us a couple of sheets of information to give us some ideas about how to train him further. Some of it was really useful, but the price we paid for her to come out for that one visit was hardly worth it; the majority of the information was things we already knew.

As Mr Fudge was now a bit older, we started to go for longer walks. He walked with me no bother at all but was still hesitant and reluctant to go with Eddie, no matter what we tried.

We followed the advice from George; I took him on boring little walks, and Eddie took him for nice long walks - a couple of miles to reduces his energy levels. But that never worked; he never stopped from the time he got up till the time we went to bed.

We decided to take him to puppy training classes. On the first visit, the instructor asked why were we here as he was sitting, staying, waiting on command. We explained about his nipping and that we wanted to get him used to other dogs. The only command he had trouble with was to lay down; he would just look at us like we were stupid and think, what are you talking about.

The trainer was Sarah, and she had done puppy training for a lot of years. Sarah suggested that we knelt down on one knee and stretched out the other leg. We then had to get Mr Fudge to come underneath the leg and say

Chapter 5. Puppy Training

the command lay down. When he did it, we were to give him a treat. This took some time for him to learn - at least a couple of weeks - but he got it in the end.

There were usually around ten other puppies in the class, but Mr Fudge only wanted to play with one of them, a little pug. He wasn't interested in any of the others at all; if they came near him, he would run back to us and sit beside my feet.

The pug felt the same towards Mr Fudge in the beginning. But soon, the pug became very popular within the class, and Mr Fudge would just sit at our feet at the end of the class playtime while the rest of the puppies ran around playing and usually chasing the little pug.

The classes went on for about eight weeks; he did so well and passed with flying colours. Sarah suggested that we try a muzzle for his nipping; when he nips, to put on the muzzle for a short time.

We went to a pet shop to look for a muzzle for Mr Fudge, and there was a square one that reminded me of Hannibal Lector's mouthpiece from Silence of the Lambs. I said no way was I getting that one, and I found a more rounded one, red and black, that looked a lot more comfortable.

Chapter 6.
Muzzle Training

I didn't want to frighten Mr Fudge with the muzzle, so I held it in one hand and a treat poking through with the other hand. I did this for a few days until Mr Fudge wasn't frightened of the muzzle. So the time came to start using it. When he started nipping, the muzzle was put on. This didn't take long as he didn't like it at all, and I didn't really like it, but it helped. He stopped nipping all the time at my arms, but he started a new thing; his barking sessions.

The barking sessions started out of the blue. He would go from 0 to 10 within seconds for no reason at all. He would get so wound up that the way we had to put a stop to it was to put him out of the room and close the door. If he barked or whimpered, we would not let him back in. He soon realised and calmed himself down, and then when he was quiet and calm, he was allowed back in.

The barking sessions started happening more each day. The more he did it, the more he got shut out, but only until he calmed down, which didn't take long, but within an hour, he would be off barking again.

Chapter 7.
The Time He Lost His Manhood

When Mr Fudge was four months old, and there was still no sign of him calming down, it became a game of wits between myself and Mr Fudge.

When Eddie and I were both off work, we would take Mr Fudge on a nice long walk around the woods for about an hour and a half. However, there was still no signs of tiring him out, even if he went on other short walks the same day, so I decided to get him some doggie agility equipment to see if this would work. I even asked Eddie's dad Brian to make Mr Fudge a seesaw.

In the garden, I set up poles for him to weave in and out of, a tunnel to go through and then the seesaw. At first, we put bricks underneath the seesaw so it didn't go up and down and scare him.

Mr Fudge absolutely loved the tunnel and the seesaw when it didn't move. To get started, I encouraged him with treats; his favourites are cheesy bites or bits of cheese.

When it came to weaving in and out of the poles, though, he looked at me as if I was stupid and just sat on the grass, refusing to move. So I got a bigger piece of cheese, and he followed me throughout the sticks, weaving as we went. However, after a while, he just refused to do any of it.

I looked into taking him to agility classes, but there were none available near us at this time.

We saw George for one of Mr Fudge's check-ups and said there was still no change, so George suggested for him to be castrated as he thought this would help calm him down. I asked if he was still too young to be castrated, but George said many dogs have been castrated at this age, and he would be fine. So a date was set for Mr Fudge's castration.

We took him to the vets in the morning, and George said he would be doing the operation.

George phoned later in the day to say it had been done and Mr Fudge was doing well. He had had ten stitches, and he would be wearing a lampshade for a few days to stop him nibbling at them.

That night we both went and picked him up; he was very pleased to see us, barking and howling and generally being very excited; George just laughed.

We got Mr Fudge home, and with the lampshade on, he was walking into everything, so we felt sorry for him and took it off. He was very good and didn't once nibble at the stitches.

Chapter 7. The Time He Lost His Manhood

After ten days, the stitches were taken out, and George said he was doing well.

Wearing his "lampshade" after losing his manhood.

Chapter 8.
Eddie's Lack of Training

As I had done all of the training with Mr Fudge, Eddie thought that Mr Fudge would do the same for him as he did for me, but Mr Fudge had other things in mind.

When I ate, Mr Fudge would be nowhere near me, but when Eddie had something to eat, Mr Fudge would be all over him. Eddie struggled to stop this from happening, so I said to Eddie, you have to put effort into training him as I can't do it for you.

Eddie had ignored what I had said until one day when he had made himself a sandwich. Mr Fudge decided he wanted a part of that sandwich, so he went up to Eddie's plate and nicked half of it. I had to leave the room as I was laughing so much.

Eddie was just shouting, "He's nicked half of my sandwich!"

I came back into the room and said again;

"you have to put the effort in to train him as I can't do it for you".

When Eddie was relaxing, sitting on the settee, and he

Chapter 8. Eddie's Lack of Training

would then get up for some reason, Mr Fudge would go to where Eddie had been sitting and lay down. When he came back, Eddie would just move along and leave Mr Fudge where he was. I said

"you have to show Mr Fudge who is the boss or he will rule you and not do anything for you".

So Eddie started to put in some effort in training Mr Fudge. Mr Fudge would do things that Eddie asked of him but not in the same way as he did for me.

Eddie would say, "I know my place; it's you, then the dog, then me."

I would just laugh, and this has never changed.

When Eddie was walking Mr Fudge, he would pull on his lead and not sit and wait to cross the road. Eddie would complain about all of this, and I would say to him, you need to train him more.

Chapter 9.
Mr Fudge's boyfriend

A friend of mine, I call her Auntie Fo, had two Jack Russells - a boy and a girl. The boy was called Brian; he and Mr Fudge loved each other. In fact, when these two went for a walk, Mr Fudge would be behind Brian and trying to mount him, Auntie Fo and I would say, get a room, you two! It was very funny but also very embarrassing at the same time.

When the time came for Brian to leave and go home, Mr Fudge would go to his bed and cry and whimper like a baby. This went on for about three hours after every visit; I think Mr Fudge was in love with his boyfriend called Brian.

Chapter 9. Mr Fudge's boyfriend

Running around the local park with best friend, Brian.

Chapter 10.
Travelling in the Car with the Crate

We bought Mr Fudge a crate to travel in the car with. We put the crate in and lowered down the back seats so he could still see us and wouldn't get too scared. He would cry initially for the first few journeys, and then after a while, we lifted one of the seats back up. Over time, all the seats in the back were put back to normal. He had now got used to travelling in the crate and settled down happily.

My friend, Auntie Fo, came round and said we should take the two dogs out for a nice long walk. However, we drove in her car to the place we were going to walk them, and she didn't have a crate in her car.

Mr Fudge had a doggy seatbelt on in the back seat of the car, and as she started to drive off, Mr Fudge started howling and barking. The noise was so intense that Fo had to stop driving; we didn't get very far. So Mr Fudge had to come onto my knee in the front seat. It was better, but he kept trying to get over onto Fo's knee.

Luckily we didn't have to go very far, and all four of us

Chapter 10. Travelling in the Car with the Crate

had a lovely walk, but this never happened again because Fo wouldn't drive Mr Fudge.

We soon realised that Mr Fudge set his own rules, and they could never be changed; he didn't like any change.

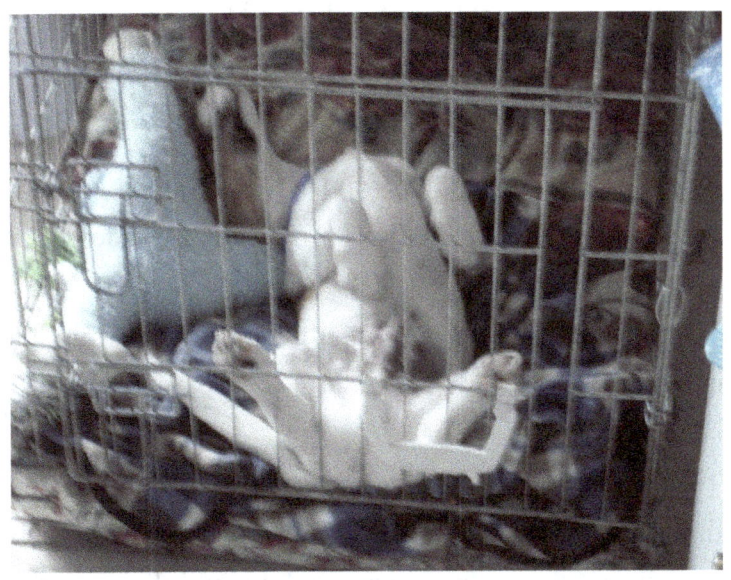

Even in his crate, asleep on his back.

Chapter 11.
The Friendship Between Mr Fudge and Auntie Fo

I made a lot of new friends from work after moving down from Northumberland to live in Yorkshire with Eddie, one of them being Auntie Fo.

Mr Fudge absolutely loves Auntie Fo. Every time she came to the house, Mr Fudge would get so excited that he peed all over her.

Not just once, but every time she came, I got the same thing: "He's pissed on me again." I would just laugh each time she said it, and the more he did it and the more she said it, the funnier I found it.

When I would say Auntie Fo is coming, Mr Fudge would sit on the arm of the corner suite, look at the window and cry until she had arrived. Mr Fudge would be going mad, so excited, barking, going round and round in circles, but his tail was the best; it would go round and round, side to side, and up and down. I thought he couldn't get any cuter.

Mr Fudge would jump all over her, trying to give her a

Chapter 11. The Friendship Between Mr Fudge and Auntie Fo

kiss. I think if he could talk, he would be saying, "I love you."

Auntie Fo would come around a lot as we worked together, and we had a really good friendship. We did a lot together, but mostly with the dogs; she would only bring Brian as her other dog was always left out in their play.

Chapter 12.
Mr Fudge's First Christmas

It's my tradition that on the first of December, Eddie would get sent into the loft to bring all the Christmas decorations and tree downstairs into the living room, where all the boxes would go on the floor.

Mr Fudge went absolutely mad, barking as they didn't belong there. He barked and growled at them for around 30 minutes until we gave him a treat to distract him.

The first thing I would do is sort out the Christmas tunes, and put them on very loud. I was decorating my window, and Mr Fudge was lying on the settee with his treat, however when a song came on that he liked, he would jump down, go to the stereo, and start howling along. I said he was singing, but at this point, Eddie would leave the room.

Then I would start working on the tree, but Mr Fudge would be into every box. His head would be in there, and I've never come across a more stubborn dog; he would not move. Instead, we would have to move the box, so I could see what I was doing.

Chapter 12. Mr Fudge's First Christmas

I have a Christmas mat to go beneath the tree, and Mr Fudge would come and sit on the mat and refuse to move. I had to pick him up and move him. Then the stand would go up, and he would be back to investigate what was going on. Every stage of the tree decorating it was the same.

When the tree was finished, we would put wrapped up empty boxes underneath the tree. Mr Fudge kept going up to them and nudging them. Then he decided to open them, so we couldn't put any presents underneath the tree as Mr Fudge would try and open all of them.

I found out the songs that he liked best were, Rocking Around the Christmas Tree, Frosty the Snowman, All I Want for Christmas, and a few more. He would sing along to all of them; it just made me laugh.

Mr Fudge had his own Advent calendar with doggy chocolate in. He picks things up very quickly; each day, he would sit there, not just looking at you but a real Paddington hard stare at you until he had your attention. We would ask what he wanted, and he would go to the door where his Advent calendar was; this happened every day.

The day before Christmas Eve, I was informed by social services that my twin grandsons were going to their new home and parents as the adoption had gone through. This broke my heart once more.

On Christmas morning, Eddie and I were in bed,

presents at the side of the bed for each of us, and I had some for Mr Fudge, who was sat at the bottom of the bed. He got so excited he jumped off the bed, running around the room, and back on the bed.

I decided to give Mr Fudge the first gift. I said Santa has been, and Mr Fudge's tail was going in all directions with excitement. Mr Fudge opened his first present; it was a new collar. Then Eddie got a present, then me, and so on and so on until there were no presents left.

Mr Fudge was so excited about his new squeaky toys, but they didn't last very long as he would chew them to get at the squeaker inside. Auntie Fo got him a small squeaky space hopper; I named it Mr Squeaky Man, as Mr Fudge knew the names of all of his toys. Mr Squeaky Man lasted around 15 days. It had stuffing inside, and once he'd made a hole in it, he was trying to eat the stuffing, so we had to take it off him.

Chapter 12. Mr Fudge's First Christmas

Mr Fudge's first Christmas.

He always enjoys opening his own presents.

Chapter 13.
Discovery of Kong Toys for Dogs

Mr Fudge would destroy every toy that he got within hours. I even went to the vets and had a chat with George to see if he had any suggestions for which would last. George gave us an all-rope toy in the shape of a bone. It was quite a thick rope, and this lasted Mr Fudge about two hours.

Most of Mr Fudge's toys didn't last five minutes, so I started doing some research, and I discovered Kong toys. The first one he had was a rugby ball, fluorescent green like the colour of a tennis ball. He managed to pull off all the green with his little sharp teeth, but the ball lasted, so, therefore, most toys we bought from then on were Kong toys.

Chapter 14.
Mr Fudge, the Andrex Dog

The bathroom in our house is downstairs, and when the bathroom door was left open, Mr Fudge would go in, jump up and reach the toilet paper. He would tear it up all over the bathroom floor and then bring it to the dining room, still on the roll, and tear it all over downstairs.

I used to say to him;

"you are not the Andrex dog! You are a Jack Russell, not a golden retriever".

The toilet roll saga went on for months; he could go through a full roll of toilet paper within seconds, so we learnt the lesson to make sure to close the bathroom door behind us. When people came to visit and left the bathroom door open, we would end up with no toilet paper left. We put a sign up on the door; please close behind you, or you will be charged for toilet paper, with a big thank you on it.

Chapter 15.
Mr Fudge and His Freckles

As I said at the start of the book, Mr Fudge only had the markings on his head, one on each side, and around his tail when we got him. Suddenly I noticed little brown freckles on his two front paws, then the next time, I noticed they were also on his back.

I said to Mr Fudge, what's happening? I got a white doggy with three markings, not with freckles.

As time has gone on, he is now covered in freckles.

Chapter 16.
Mr Fudge Turns One Year Old

They say when a dog is jumping around you and barking, that you should ignore it, but if you did this with Mr Fudge, he just wouldn't stop.

I would try turning my back to him, with my arms folded, but he would jump up and nip my arse with his front teeth. It really hurt, so this technique never worked with Mr Fudge.

We tried all sorts of techniques, including the clicker training method; he would bark at it every single time. Mr Fudge has his own mind, and he just does what he wants to do. He would demand your attention, and keep doing this until I reacted and turned around and said, "You little fucker," as my arse really hurt and was covered in bruises.

I read and watched many dog training DVDs and books, and they all say the same things, but not one thing worked with him to stop him from demanding your attention. This carried on for about two years, and then one day, he just stopped and found a new way to outwit me.

Chapter 17.
Family Visit

One of my brothers came to visit along with his family. Mr Fudge has been trained not to go near our food, but he thinks other people's is fair game, which we were not aware of.

When my brother came through the front door, the first thing he said was, "Where is my bacon sandwich?"

I was expecting this, so I was already frying the bacon. I served them the sandwiches as they sat at our dining room table. As he was sitting down, his grandson called him away, so he stood back up, leaving the chair out from under the table.

Mr Fudge saw his opportunity. Quick as a flash, he was up on the chair, and the next thing we know is my brother shouting, "He's nicked off with my sandwich, the little fucker!"

Eddie was standing in the doorway, absolutely pissing himself laughing. Mr Fudge flew out the back door into the garden, thoroughly enjoying his sandwich.

Chapter 18.
Wedding Plans

Believe this or not, but to organise our wedding day didn't take me very long, as I knew exactly what we wanted, where we wanted to be married and who were going to be our guests. The only thing I could not arrange was Mr Fudge being the ring bearer, as no dogs were allowed in the registry office.

When Eddie got down on one knee and proposed to me, Mr Fudge was in the middle of us, jumping up at Eddie as Mr Fudge was wondering what Eddie was up to and thought he must be wanting to play with him.

Within three days, I had the day, the photographer, the flowers, our wedding reception venue and the registry office all booked and paid for.

As Eddie doesn't really like or feel comfortable in big crowds, we only invited two friends each, plus our two immediate families, to the actual wedding. One of Eddie's guests, Stephen and David, would be his best man, and Trish and Brad were my guests.

All of our friends and extended family came to our

evening reception; we also had a honeymoon booked and paid for on the Isle of Mull in Scotland.

I'm not one for doing things the old, traditional way, so the only things we decided to use were something old, something new, something borrowed and something blue. We aren't religious, and the last thing we wanted was lots of prayers and hymns. That's why we chose the registry office, as we could pick what parts and words of the service we wanted.

I said to Eddie I didn't want to waste any money on a big fancy car, and neither did he on all the other stuff that goes along with the wedding. We decided the something new was my wedding dress and Eddies suit; something borrowed was a tiara that matched the colours of my dress; something old was my imam's charm bracelet, she died when I was in my 20s, and it was important to me to have something that meant so much to her when she was alive, and something blue was a garter that I wore.

Trish is one of my best mates. I've known her for years as we worked together when I lived in Northumberland for a long time, and Brad is her husband. Stephen and David have known Eddie since they were children. He couldn't decide which would be best man, so he had both.

I have quite a large family; my dad, two sisters, and two brothers with all of their families. Eddies family is his mum

Chapter 18. Wedding Plans

and dad plus one brother with his wife and family; altogether, there were nine adults and 11 children. I decided not to have any bridesmaids as it would not be fair on the others. My dad was too unwell to give me away, so I asked my oldest brother.

We thought about Mr Fudge on the day; we couldn't leave him alone all this time, so we decided to take him with us in the car for the actual ceremony. He would happily settle down asleep in his crate.

In between the ceremony and the reception we took Mr Fudge with us to have our photographs taken in a beautiful woodland nearby and at the same time, Mr Fudge could have a nice run.

Trish and Brad asked if they could make our wedding cake as a gift for us both. The day before the ceremony, Trish and Brad travelled down from Northumberland to stay with us and brought the wedding cake. My God, it was fantastic! It was a castle; I love castles and go all over visiting them.

On the day of the ceremony, as it wasn't until 2 pm, Trish, Brad, and I took Mr Fudge for a nice long walk in the morning. The sun was shining, it was a beautiful day, and Eddie was at home waiting for the flowers to arrive.

We got back home around 10:30 and started to get ready. I had a bath whilst music was playing; one of the tunes was The Final Countdown, which I thought was really funny. Trish helped me into my dress, and Brad helped out with the flowers. It was arranged for Stephen, David and both of our families to meet us at the registry office. Eddie and I travelled with Mr Fudge in our own car, Trish and Brad followed in theirs.

When we entered the registry office, we had to go into the office one at a time to be asked some final questions. Eddie was first, then went to wait in the ceremony room while I answered my questions and got ready for my entrance.

The music started, and I made my way up to Eddie. Then the registrar who was performing the service asked where my bouquet was; I'd only gone and left it on the office desk.

"Can we do it again?" I asked.

"Of course," she said.

So, back out I went for attempt two, this time with the flowers. Eddie had to explain to the guests what was happening as not all had seen. The ceremony lasted around 20 minutes, and the photographer was there taking photos.

Afterwards, we went to the Woodlands, with everyone following us in their own cars. Eddie and I took Mr Fudge for a quick walk around; yes, I was still in my wedding dress. The photo-taking took around 2 hours, then all of

Chapter 18. Wedding Plans

our families and friends went off to the reception hotel as they were staying there overnight.

Eddie and I went back home to drop off Mr Fudge. Mr Fudge sat on the train of my wedding dress as I walked from room to room; he enjoyed being pulled along. I had to laugh at him and said, "

it's my dress, you little four-legged shit bag".

Making sure he was settled, we left for the evening reception.

The reception was amazing; we ended up doing two first dances, as some guests didn't arrive till later as they were working later shifts. Eddie's not a dancer and hates attention, but he got through it.

After the party, we went back home to see to Mr Fudge.

Eddie went to the hotel the next morning as he wanted to pick up the leftover food, cake and flowers and balloons from the tables: typical Yorkshireman.

Chapter 19.
Mr Fudge Chewing Through His Harness

From Mr Fudge being a puppy, we used a non-pull harness with the lead attached. Mr Fudge, while walking, would be jumping up and biting on his lead; he was so excited to be out.

After about six months, he had chewed through his first harness. We bought the same type of harness, and again, three months later, he chewed through that one as well.

So we bought a different kind of harness with a separate lead, and he chewed through the lead within weeks.

We had to find a way to stop him from chewing through his lead. I thought I would buy a leather one to see if this would work, but he just chewed through it.

So, in the end, I found a really thick lead, and although he tried, he didn't manage to chew through it. Finally, this stopped him from chewing any more leads.

Chapter 20.
My Hairdresser

My hairdresser is called Elizabeth, and she first did my hair before our wedding. We are not far apart in age and hit it off straight away. When Elizabeth does my hair, she does like to try fluff it up, but I'm not the kind of person to have fluffy hair, so I keep telling her no fluffing. She just laughs at me and says

"I'm sorry, I'll put the hairbrush down".

Elizabeth did a fantastic job of my hair for the wedding. When Elizabeth first arrived, Mr Fudge decided to go through her bag, and he found a notebook that he thought was something to rip up. There was paper all over the floor! All I could do was apologise, but Elizabeth just laughed.

Mr Fudge absolutely adores her. When I tell him that Elizabeth is coming, he goes round in a circle, then clonks himself on the sofa, watching the window for her to arrive. He whines and cries like a baby. Every time a car passes, he jumps up, runs to the living room door and near howls. He's so excited, and this goes on, even if there is no one there. So I've learnt only to tell him 15 minutes before she comes.

Chapter 21.
Mr Fudge's First Holiday and Our Honeymoon

We set off around 6 am to head to Oban. We knew it was going to be a long drive, and Eddie had sorted out a few stops for a break and to give Mr Fudge a chance to get out of the car.

First stop was the Llama Karma cafe, not far from Carlisle. It's a cafe which also has all kinds of animals: llamas, chickens, budgies and other kinds of birds and small mammals. There was a nice little walk up to the Countess Pillar, and there was a wooden statue outside. We took Mr Fudge on this walk before we went into the cafe, making sure that he had water and the window guards were on the car so he could get some fresh air through. Inside, it was a really nice place to stop; we could go outside and pets the llamas after we'd had some coffee.

Back in the car, we travelled on for another hour to the next stop, which was where we'd planned to have our lunch. It's called Annandale Water, near Lockerbie. This place was absolutely amazing; it had a beautiful walk around a lake

Chapter 21. Mr Fudge's First Holiday and Our Honeymoon

and was very dog friendly, but no dogs were allowed inside. We had our own packed lunch, but we bought teas and coffees. Mr Fudge had his own lunch, and we spent around one and a half hours there.

We then drove on for another three hours to get past Glasgow and up towards the Highlands. For our next stop, we just pulled into a roadside rest stop.

We arrived in Oban around 6 pm. We were meant to be staying at a dog-friendly bed and breakfast, which was booked at the same time as the wedding. However, on arrival, I went and knocked at the door, and we were told we couldn't stay as there had been a death in the family. The people from the bed and breakfast hadn't contacted us, so we didn't know. We had to phone around and find somewhere else to stay.

The only place we could find at short notice for that night was a pub which also had rooms. It wasn't the best place we've stayed by a long way; as you walked across the carpet, your feet stuck to it. The only clean place was the bathroom. There was a car park at the top of the street, and we didn't even unpack the car fully, just took out what we needed and anything valuable. It cost around £60 for the one night, with breakfast on top for another £10 each.

We went for a walk around Oban with Mr Fudge to look for somewhere to eat. We ended up having fish and chips, and Mr Fudge had two sausages without batter. It was very nice sitting by the harbour, eating fish and chips.

We continued our walk around Oban and, as we were walking down the street by the harbour where all the shops are, Mr Fudge was in front of us on his lead. I saw something which looked like a small dead octopus lying on the path, but before I could pull Mr Fudge away, he had gobbled it up! I don't even think he'd chewed it; it was gone. I thought, what the hell was that he's just eaten? All we could do was hope that he would be fine; we had our fingers crossed as we were only there overnight.

Mr Fudge barked throughout the night, whenever he heard people coming and going from the pub, so we didn't get much sleep.

We woke around 4:30 and didn't feel like staying for breakfast there, so we literally had a quick cuppa and left.

We went down to the harbour to find out where the ferry terminal was. As Oban has several one-way streets, I said to Eddie we should walk it and find the way to the ferry. We found our way and went back to move the car so we could park it at the terminal, ready for our ferry at 10:30. We'd seen a Tesco supermarket nearby that was open 24 hours and had a cafe that was already open.

We had a beautiful full English breakfast for much cheaper than the pub would have cost and bought a few

Chapter 21. Mr Fudge's First Holiday and Our Honeymoon

things that we needed to get started when we arrived at the cottage as we were self-catering.

Time soon passed, and we were ready to board the ferry. We had no idea how Mr Fudge would react to being onboard. There were certain seats that were dog friendly on the decks. The sun was shining, and it was nice and warm. We found seats, and I tied his lead to the bottom of the chair; he still had room to move about or sit on our knees. The people behind us fell in love with Mr Fudge; they said he was so cute and well-behaved. My answer was "you wouldn't be saying that if you lived with him, he's a fucking little shit"; they just laughed.

Mr Fudge absolutely loved the ferry ride; he was so good, enjoying the spray of the water, we saw some dolphins swimming close by. It was amazing.

Mr Fudge: The Naughtiest Dog Ever

Enjoying a walk around the lake at Annandale Water.

Chapter 22.
The Isle of Mull

After we docked in Craignure, we drove off the ferry. Eddie had the sat-nav already set up, and off we went to find our cottage. It wasn't far out of town until we turned off onto a small road that was shaped like a horseshoe; we were in the detached cottage right at the end of the row. I can't tell you how stunning the views were over the sea loch, Loch Don.

Our cottage was built in the 18th-century; it was small and cosy and had a massive garden with trees and a small brick wall around. It had two floors; upstairs, below the V-shaped sloping ceiling, was one very large room, but it was two bedrooms. At one side, there was a double bed and a cot in the central area where the staircase was; then, at the other end of the cottage, there were two single beds with a curtain that pulled across to separate the sleeping areas. There was a window in the ceiling, a set of drawers and a wardrobe on the side with the double bed. Under the drawers, there was a biggish TV, but it had no signal. We stored our suitcase and bags on the opposite side, where the two beds were.

Downstairs, in the living room, there was a fireplace with a log burner and three shelves filled with books and DVDs. There was a TV on the wall and a round metal table. In front of the fireplace, there was a wooden table with a glass surface and a pink three-piece suite with a chair.

Across the room, the bathroom was downstairs, and it was very yellow. The kitchen was a large square with everything we would need: fridge, freezer, washing machine, tumble dryer and others like cooker and microwave and other necessities, e.g. iron and ironing board. It had a breakfast table in there set up with a small welcome pack of a loaf of bread, butter, milk, plus kindling and logs for the fire. Attached to the kitchen was a utility room, where you could dry washing and store muddy boots.

Outside the cottage at the front, facing the sea loch, was a metal seat made for two. I called it the old gadgee seat. There was a mesh fence surrounding the front of the cottage on top of the small boundary wall. The garden was huge and all grass with one outbuilding behind the cottage. The garden in this area sloped upwards quite steeply towards a row of trees.

After we unloaded the car and got settled in, we had a cup of tea and coffee. As we sat on the seat admiring the scenery looking out over the loch, we heard some kind of

Chapter 22. The Isle of Mull

insect flying by. Mr Fudge had the whole of the garden to run around while it was light, but when it became dark, and we could not see him, he would be put on his extendible lead as neither of us fancied playing hunt the dog in the pitch black of night. We were there for seven days, and it's one of the most beautiful places we've ever stayed; so peaceful and tranquil.

One of the rules on the Isle of Mull is that cattle can roam free. One evening as it was getting dusk, we had all these hairy cows coming, happily wandering down the little lane. Mr Fudge was in the garden, and he saw the hairy cows standing near the fence. I've never seen him move so fast; he came and sat next to me on the old gadgee seat. Some of the cows seem to be interested in Mr Fudge, and they bent over the fence, watching him for a while. Mr Fudge moved closer to me and just stared at the cows, and the cows stared at Mr Fudge; it was really funny.

I woke up early one morning to find we had sheep - a whole flock of them - wandering along the lane.

Other rules I found out were that, in Scotland, there is the Right to Roam, which means you can park a camper van or pitch a tent virtually anywhere. There are of course also plenty of proper sites where you paid and had all the facilities you would need. A lot of land on the island is quite cheap as trees had been planted for timber plantations but were only shallow-rooted and needed to be felled safely; if you bought the land, you had to clear the trees.

We had a fabulous honeymoon, exploring the Island with Mr Fudge, doing wildlife safaris and visiting stunning beaches. One of the small beaches on the small island of Iona looked just like the Caribbean, with gorgeous clear blue sea and white sand.

The holiday cottage on the Isle of Mull.

Chapter 22. The Isle of Mull

Sat on the old gadgee seat, watching the herd of cows that appeared.

Investigating a jellyfish at Calgary Bay on the Isle of Mull.

Chapter 23.
Learning How to Knit

I decided I wanted to learn how to knit. Auntie Fo was a really good knitter, so I got instructions and lessons from her.

I went into our local market where I knew a lady called Jan, who sold wool, all sorts of fabrics and general bric-a-brac. Mr Fudge and I were patiently queueing behind a couple that were looking at some things on Jan's stall. Mr Fudge was in front of me on his lead, and I was minding my own business, waiting to be served.

The couple in front had a rucksack, unzipped on the floor, and Mr Fudge decided to have a nosey inside. I looked down and saw his head inside this rucksack - I think they had some sausage rolls or pasties inside. I pulled Mr Fudge back from the rucksack, and he had grabbed whatever was in the paper bag and eaten it in one gulp, leaving the empty paper bag behind!

I said I didn't feel him move on the lead. I couldn't believe he did it; I didn't even hear any rustling of the paper bag. All I could do was apologise, and I kept saying I'm

Chapter 23. Learning How to Knit

really sorry.

The couple quickly paid for their things, picked up the rucksack and left. Jan was rolling around laughing.

I bought a large ball of wool and knitting needles as I was going to try and make knit myself a new hat.

When I got home, I thought I would start knitting, but Mr Fudge had other things in mind; he picked up the wool and ran outside into the garden. I was chasing him; there was wool everywhere - he unravelled near enough the whole ball. I tried to untangle it, but it was so knotted I had to put the whole mess in the bin.

So off we went back to Jan's to buy another ball of wool. Jan just peed herself with laughter when I told her what Mr Fudge had done.

Soon after, Jan moved into a shop in the main shopping street. Her shop is on two floors; the downstairs is the wool shop, and upstairs are house clearance items. Mr Fudge and I often call into Jan's shop for wool, but when Mr Fudge sees the wool, he yanks me on his lead to try and get at it.

To this day, we often have a natter and many conversations about Mr Fudge and how he attacks the wool with me at home and her shop.

Chapter 24.
Mr Fudge Comfort Suckling

I can't remember when Mr Fudge started with his comfort suckling, but I do remember how he started it. I must admit I love being in pyjamas and my onesie or dressing gown on my days off. When I had a onesie or dressing gown on, Mr Fudge started to knead with his feet and suck on the soft material of the dressing gown or onesie. Where he tried to start was my breasts.

I don't know why he started, but I used to have to sit with my hands over my boobs until he would go and knead and suck somewhere else, lower down. It took a few weeks for Mr Fudge to get the message that he wasn't going to suckle near my boobs.

He still suckles to this day, either on my belly or the top of my leg, which I don't mind. I just have to have a clean dressing gown or onesie each time as he soaks it when he sucks on the material. I end up with some wet patches down my leg and around my belly area.

I researched and believe the reason behind this behaviour is because he was weaned too soon from his mother. Other people say it's a comfort thing and/or if they're feeling scared, but I personally think he was weaned far too early.

Mr Fudge Comfort Suckling.

Chapter 25.
No More Cushions

Eddie is what I would call a computer geek.

One day, while I was at work, he was upstairs in the computer room, and Mr Fudge was downstairs, being very quiet. Eddie thought nothing of it, thinking he might be asleep, but when he came downstairs, he couldn't believe his eyes. Mr Fudge had only gone and eaten all the stuffing in my cushions!

He'd scratched the material on the outside till there was a great big hole in it, then pulled out and eaten the stuffing leaving the material on the outside.

Not just one - he ate all four of them, the little bastard! Eddie couldn't believe his eyes; yet again, not one bit of stuffing left.

Mr Fudge was rushed to the vets, who had a good look at him and said he's fine, just keep an eye on him.

Chapter 26.
Charlotte the Vet

Mr Fudge has, for as long as I can remember, had a thing for eating grass, and when he was really young, he used to eat moss. Mr Fudge used to go to the vets every 28 days to have tablets to protect him against lungworm because of all the grass he eats.

Charlotte the vet could do anything with Mr Fudge. He would still be happily wagging his tail while she was emptying his glands, or with a finger up his bottom, or taking his temperature. He never flinched one bit; Charlotte could do whatever she wanted with him.

If George went to do any of this, Mr Fudge would growl, lie down and make it very hard for George to do anything.

Mr Fudge mostly used to see Charlotte for his lungworm tablet.

Every 28 days, I would say, "We are off to see Charlotte." He would get very excited, run around in circles and chase his tail.

Chapter 27.
Bugs in His Lugs

I noticed one afternoon when I came in from work and Eddie had been off all day that Mr Fudge was crying when he went to scratch his ears, which we Geordie's call his lugs. I asked Eddie if he'd noticed anything, but he hadn't. Mr Fudge had just laid down and slept most of the day.

I was on an early the next day, so I made an appointment to see George in the afternoon, and Mr Fudge and I walked up to the vets for his consultation.

George tried to look inside Mr Fudge's ears, but they were red and angry and a bit swollen inside.

George said he would have to knock him out to have a proper look to see what was going on.

An appointment was arranged for us to take him in at 9 in the morning, then George would ring later to let us what he had found.

George phoned us in the afternoon to say that he had found ear mites, but we could pick him up later that day.

In the evening, when we arrived to pick up Mr Fudge, George met us and said

Chapter 27. Bugs in His Lugs

"he has been howling to the music throughout the afternoon";

I just laughed. George said he needed to have ear drops and dog food that was soft for his stomach, as he'd been sedated. I asked how he could have caught the mites, and George said from long grasses and shrubs.

Chapter 28.
Mr Fudge Becomes Unwell

As you gather from what you've read already, this dog does not stop and is always into mischief.

Suddenly, with no pattern, mostly on a weekly basis, he started vomiting a couple of times a day. I took him to the vets, and we saw George; he couldn't find anything wrong with him.

This went on for a few months, going back and forwards to the vets and seeing different vets. George asked us to keep a record of when he refused to eat food that day or vomited, and we kept this diary for a few weeks.

I could tell Mr Fudge was not himself at all; he was just lying around, not wanting to play and not eating for a couple of days. I made an appointment to see George and said

"there is something really wrong with him - we need to find out what it is";

George agreed. He took blood samples and a scan of his belly.

The scan showed that he had a hardening of the

Chapter 28. Mr Fudge Becomes Unwell

stomach wall, and the bloods came back with an illness called pancreatitis. George said that this can be very painful in humans and animals, but animals can't tell us.

Mr Fudge has always had loads of fur loss, constantly shedding; you can hoover up one minute, and within seconds, there is hair everywhere again.

Mr Fudge had some really bad flare up episodes of his pancreatitis, and he ended up in doggy hospital - staying at the vet's surgery - a few times over the years. Mr Fudge was put on a low-fat diet which meant no more treats for him. After a while, he did go back on a few treats that we knew didn't affect him.

Mr Fudge has had many different medications to try and help his condition. In all of these years, there's one that has not changed, and that's called Lypex. This is a capsule, but we can't get him to swallow it, so we split it in two and sprinkle the contents on his food. He has one and a half of these a day.

Chapter 29.
Trying to Clean the House

As soon as I got the Hoover out, Mr Fudge would try to kill it. He would be biting the head and barking at it; you couldn't get moved as he would be in your way.

The only way Mr Fudge would leave the Hoover, sweeping brush and hand brush alone, was to hold a treat in your hands. Then he would sit and ignore the Hoover… But, if you gave him the treat, he'd start again. I quickly learnt to hang onto the treat until I had finished.

Now dusting was a different matter. Mr Fudge would sit and watch me for around five minutes, and then he decided to come and pinch the duster from my hands. He'd run away with it, sometimes under the dining room table or, if the back-door was open, out into the garden.

Chapter 30.
I Can't Believe It – He's Four Years Old!

Life is moving along as it does, passing quickly, and Mr Fudge, on good days, is up to his same old mischief.

Mr Fudge has now stopped being the Andrex dog, and "behind enemy lines" have all come down. I can finally say, after four years, he is showing signs of calming down. You can't say it didn't take very long, ha.

Mr Fudge is four years old. As this year was coming to an end, we thought he'd started to grow out of all the naughty stuff.

How wrong we were.

Chapter 31.
Mr Fudge's Trying to Hump My Arm

Every time the house phone rings and I am in, Mr Fudge jumps up on the sofa and tries to hump my arm as I'm trying to answer the phone. I'm sure he's jealous and trying to get my attention away from the person I'm talking to on the phone and back onto him.

This dog is so demanding, and he gets very jealous when I'm talking on the phone, as he can't see who I'm talking to, and he doesn't like it.

When I tell him to get down, he goes round in a circle and jumps back up at my arm, humping it. First of all, I have to apologise to the person I'm talking to, move the handset away from my head, and then tell Mr Fudge

"I will crack his arse"

if he doesn't get down. He just looks at me like I'm stupid.

Mr Fudge does not give up easily; this goes on throughout the phone call, and in the end, I end up calling him a little fucker. I go to smack his leg, he goes to run away

Chapter 31. Mr Fudge's Trying to Hump My Arm

but comes back barking at me and then the fucking little twat nips me with his front teeth. I end up yelping, then he runs away and yet again, I have a bruise on my arm.

Chapter 32.
Deciding on the New Shed

When we moved into this property a few years ago, at the bottom of the garden, there was a wooden shed. The shed was now not in the best condition, so we decided it was time for a replacement. We use it as a utility room, and our freezers and dryer are in it.

Eddie and I were talking about what kind of shed we would get. Eddie did a bit of research, and we went to have a look at some different garden centres, but we didn't see anything that we wanted. After further discussion, I came up with a suggestion of a metal shed. At first, Eddie wasn't keen, so I said to him,

"you are not getting any younger, and if we get a metal shed, you will never have to paint it again".

So we looked around at metal sheds, finding one online; the price and size were right.

Eddie isn't mechanical minded, but we do have relations that are very handy tradespeople, general builders, carpenters, etc. The one we called on was Eddie's cousin, Chris, who is a builder.

Chapter 32. Deciding on the New Shed

Now Mr Fudge accepts anyone coming into the house through the front door as we have let them in. Chris had been to the house before and knew Mr Fudge very well, always making a big fuss of him. So when we asked Chris if he could put together our new shed, he agreed, and the cost and dates were agreed.

The day came when Chris was going to make a start on the shed. However, instead of parking at the front of the house, Chris parked at the back, near where the old shed was to be dismantled and the new one erected, and he came through our back gate. Halfway down our garden, we have a small brick wall with a gate that partitions off the grass area nearest the house from the gravel area where the shed is.

Mr Fudge is on the lawned area when Chris comes in through the back gates, and he goes absolutely mental as people don't usually come in that way. He was growling, baring his teeth and barking; the noise was unbearable. After talking to Mr Fudge and saying it was only Chris, the growling and the teeth-baring stopped, but the barking continued.

So after what felt like hours of this, I said to Chris,

"for Pete's sake, come and say hello to him, so he knows who you are, and then, hopefully, he'll shut up".

Chris walks through the little garden gate, and Mr

Fudge goes bonkers. He starts to chase Chris around the garden; all I could do was laugh until Mr Fudge nipped him on the ankle. Luckily Chris had work boots on, but he said, you fucking little bastard!

Within two minutes, Mr Fudge had worked out who it was and was all over him.

It took Chris three days to demolish the old shed and put together the new one. Each day when Chris came through the back gates, Mr Fudge would go to the garden gate, wagging his tail, say hello, and he never barked or growled at Chris again.

Chapter 33.
Holiday to Dover and Mr Fudge's Most Stressful Time

We didn't know just how stressed Mr Fudge could get. We found this out on holiday in St Margaret's Bay near Dover. We were so looking forward to it; all the history and all the castles we were going to visit.

We arrived a bit too early to book into the cottage we were staying in, so we decided to go for a look round, and we ended up at the beach. Underneath the white cliffs, the beaches were all pebbled but with beautiful scenery, and it was a lovely sunny day.

After a walk to exercise Mr Fudge and stretch our legs, it was time to find the cottage, which was located at St Margaret's Bay Holiday Park. We hadn't really taken much notice of the facilities surrounding our cottage when we booked; we just thought it would be a cottage on the site.

The weather was red-hot; it was 33° for the whole week we were there. We usually took a pen for Mr Fudge so he could be outside but secure if needed. He hadn't been in the pen for a couple of years, but we always had it with us - just in case.

Mr Fudge had always enjoyed our holidays, except for the place we stayed this time. He did not like the cottage at all, and we did not understand why; he had everything he needed, or so we thought.

We got ourselves unpacked, had a drink and went off to do some shopping as we were self-catering. We saw a pet shop and bought Mr Fudge one of the screw-in poles with a long lead that you screw into the grass, thinking it would give him a bit more freedom than the pen.

When we got back to the cottage, we screwed his lead into the grass. He had plenty of lead so he could go where we wanted to within the space we had. He could come into the cottage or lie on the grass; there was a table and chairs outside that catered for four people, and he had plenty lead to reach us while we sat outside.

The cottage had two double bedrooms, a small kitchen, a medium-sized bathroom and a small lounge area. It was probably more of a brick-built chalet than what you think of as a cottage.

Mr Fudge became really stressed, and he would just be pacing back-and-forth, not settling at all outside. He only settled while we were in bed, and he was inside with us. We tried to encourage him to play with his toys, but he didn't want to know, which was quite unusual for Mr Fudge.

Chapter 33. Holiday to Dover and Mr Fudge's Most Stressful Time

When we were out for the day, Mr Fudge was so happy he would be rolling on the grass, which he loves to do, and just being his normal, happy self. We went to Dover Castle, the battlefield of Hastings, Deal Castle, and Hever Castle.

At Dover Castle, we did the outside areas first, knowing that Mr Fudge was not allowed inside the main keep or wartime tunnels. The outside took most of the day to see everything, and Mr Fudge absolutely loved it. He was rolling in the grass and saying hello to all the other people walking around the grounds.

A couple of days later, we went back to go inside the keep and the wartime tunnels; it really is an absolutely amazing place to see.

We'd left Mr Fudge secure in the cottage that day as it was so hot, and there would have been nowhere to leave him in the castle while we were inside. He was safe and in a nice cool place. We removed all of the cushions and anything that had stuffing inside, putting them in the bedroom and making the door was securely closed. Then we put his pen across the main patio doors and closed the curtains.

In the evenings, we would have the patio doors open and his pen across the doorway to let air through and cool the room down while keeping Mr Fudge secure.

Another hot day we went to the battlefield of Hastings.

I really thought, this is going to be shit, but in fact, it was the opposite. It was fantastic. Battle Abbey and walking around the battlefield listening to the audio tour was brilliant. It is a day out I would recommend to anyone; there is so much to do, and best of all, you can play with a lot of stuff. Mr Fudge could be with us for it was very dog friendly; the cafe had tables outside where we could eat with Mr Fudge.

Inside there is a museum spread over four floors, all to do with the Battle of Hastings. My favourite floor was filled with shields that you could use to take photos with; I love a dress up.

There were ruins of the abbey; you could go in and out of every nook and cranny, and so could Mr Fudge. There is a big plaque on the floor where King Harold died during the Battle of Hastings in 1066. I must say, I absolutely loved it.

We all really enjoyed this holiday, although it was so hot I had to go on and buy some new clothes. I'd packed for more typical British weather, but it was 33° all week.

We discussed with George when we got home how stressed Mr Fudge had been. George thought it might have been too open on the holiday camp; he didn't know where the boundary was for our area, so he was on guard for the whole site.

Chapter 33. Holiday to Dover and Mr Fudge's Most Stressful Time

We learnt a lesson about Mr Fudge going on holiday. Now when we booked our holidays, the first thing we look for is a fully enclosed garden, so Mr Fudge has a stress-free holiday.

We have had many more holidays as the years have gone by; Mr Fudge has loved them all with his enclosed garden to himself.

The holiday cottage at St Margaret's Bay near Dover.

Making himself at home at St Margaret's Bay.

Looking out the patio doors at St Margaret's Bay, the start of a stressful time.

Chapter 33. Holiday to Dover and Mr Fudge's Most Stressful Time

Enjoying a good roll at Dover Castle.

Finding a bit of shade at Hever Castle on a very hot day.

Mr Fudge: The Naughtiest Dog Ever

Another good roll while walking around Battle battlefield.

Chapter 34.
Keeping Mr Fudge Well and George's Retirement

It's been very hard to get Mr Fudge's medication down him. We have tried all kinds of ways that you can think of to get him to swallow a tablet, but he just spits them back out. We've tried peanut butter, big blocks of cheese, in with his tinned food, put it in his mouth, hold his mouth closed and rub his throat, but none of this works for us. Now we crush any pills or open capsules and sprinkle the contents in with food, usually chicken, which is Mr Fudge's favourite; it's working for now.

When George announced that he was retiring, I was absolutely gutted, but I understood after he told me that his dad died young and had only had a few months after his retirement, so he wanted to enjoy more of his.

Before he finished, he organised for his practice to merge with another local one, rather than be consumed by a large national one. The one that George merged with is the one I left before I went to his. I was a bit unsure as I'd not been too happy with them before, but George said I could ask to see vets from his team. I did, and it worked for a time.

Mr Fudge became ill, and I was told by a vet from the other team that they weren't going to take him in to stay, but I knew he was not well. The vet didn't want to listen to me; they treated him and wanted to send him home. I know my dog, when he's ok to come home and when he needs to be kept in doggy hospital, so I told the vet he needed to be kept in, or we would end up rushing him in the next day. They relented and agreed to keep him in for a night's observation.

The next day, I had a phone call with the same vet; they said he has got worse overnight and that I had been right. I decided at this point that when George retired, I was going to change vets.

Chapter 35.
George's Retirement Day

I have a friend who makes beautiful cakes, so I asked her to make me one as my farewell to George along with some gifts.

The cake turned out beautifully. It had Mr Fudge's face on it from a photo with his Christmas hat on. It was red with a pom-pom on and holes and each side for his ears to come out, and it tied underneath his chin. The photo had won a Christmas competition in the vet's practice.

I went to see George and say my goodbyes. I told him

"he was the best vet that I've ever known, and I hope he enjoys his long retirement".

One of his daughters is a veterinarian nurse, and she still works at the Practice. I cannot not mention the rest of the team that George had; they were all fantastic, from the receptionist all the way to the vets. I won't forget any of them.

Mr Fudge: The Naughtiest Dog Ever

The cake I had made for George's retirement.

Chapter 36.
Finding a New Vets

I did a lot of homework on all the vets in our area. A new one had just been built in a nearby town, and one of the owners years ago was George's partner, so I went and had a chat with them to see what I thought. I explained that I needed the vets to listen to me, as I knew Mr Fudge very well. I explained that I was waiting for George to retire and then I would be coming to join them.

I made the phone call to George's surgery, and I spoke to the receptionist named Kim. I really liked her; nothing was ever too much bother. Kim said she was very sad that we were leaving, but we would be welcome back at any time.

So Mr Fudge joined the new vets. Mr Fudge is still becoming unwell; he is still being sick, not eating some days and ending up in doggy hospital when his condition flares up because of his pancreatitis.

He became really unwell once but showed some slightly different symptoms. He was losing a lot more fur, unable to lie on his belly and crying in pain. So we went to see his new vet, Toby, who ran some tests and discovered that Mr Fudge had an acute case of Addison's disease. He explained that's why Mr Fudge had become bloated and was experiencing fur loss. His stress levels had become so high that with the condition, he could no longer control his own body temperature.

Mr Fudge ended up staying in doggy hospital for around five days; this is the longest he's ever had to stay in.

When we found out about Addison's disease, it explained a lot about Mr Fudge - why he got stressed, his fur loss and constant shedding.

Toby had been in contact with a specialist, and they discussed how to move forward with Mr Fudge's condition. He was put on a low dose of steroids, plus having an injection of Colvasone once every 28 days. This was followed by a blood test 10 days later to monitor his reaction.

It took time to get the dose of the steroid and Colvasone injection right. Mr Fudge had the injection for over a year, and the amount got reduced until it was not worth administering to him anymore. Toby and the consultant both agreed to stop the injection but to carry on with the steroids and other medication.

To this day, I have not yet met all of the staff that work at this vets, but their reputation is fantastic. The whole

Chapter 36. Finding a New Vets

team is phenomenal, and at the time of writing this, they have been joined by Peter Wright from the Yorkshire Vet TV series.

With Toby the vet at Grace Lane.

Epilogue.
Where We Are Now: Mr Fudge Is Nine Years Old

Mr Fudge still tries to outwit me in every way, still tries to hump my arm when I'm on the house phone, and still has his barking sessions where he has to be locked out of the room.

This book has all been done from my memory, and yes, I've most likely forgotten some small things that he got up to, but I hope you get the idea.

In our living room, I have a lot of mediaeval knight figures around the room, and there are some on the floor next to our TV stand. Mr Fudge likes to nudge them with his nose every day, then just stands there looking at them to see if they move. He can stand there for 10 minutes just watching them. This is really funny; his head goes to one side, and I just laugh.

Mr Fudge now tries to nudge everything, including the washing machine, ironing board, coffee table, my games console and of course, all of my mediaeval knights.

Mr Fudge has helped me through one of the most

Epilogue. Where We Are Now: Mr Fudge Is Nine Years Old

difficult times of my life. All of the antics and the trouble he's got into and all of the name-calling has helped me move on and get by. It just shows you how much a dog knows what you need in the time you need it.

Mr Fudge truly is my four-legged hero, alongside Eddie, whose support and love has meant I've made it through these years with a smile on my face.

In the last two years, where we've had to deal with the COVID-19 global pandemic, all the lockdowns and all the sadness, I just wanted to make you smile or even giggle when reading about this naughty little dog.

I am proud to say I am a key worker for the NHS.

Chilled out on another holiday.

In front of Salisbury Cathedral.

Epilogue. Where We Are Now: Mr Fudge Is Nine Years Old

Naughty boy, drinking from the font in Salisbury Cathedral.

We decided he had to do some time in the stocks for the font drinking.

In loving memory of my father-in-law, "Bri."
17th September 1938 to 19th November 2019.

About the Author

Sarah Reynold is a Geordie, born in North Shields, Northumberland.

In her late teens, she moved to London before moving back to her native Northumberland in her thirties.

She then moved to North Yorkshire to live with her now-husband Eddie. Sarah has worked as a caregiver for both the elderly and individuals with special needs, and she currently works for the NHS in a dementia unit.

www.ingramcontent.com/pod-product-compliance
Lightning Source LLC
Chambersburg PA
CBHW070938080526
44589CB00013B/1556